W9-AVY-795

THE FULFILLMENT FACTOR

MICHAEL KENDRICK

Acknowledgements

I would like to thank both Shana Schutte and Ben Ortlip, who each have helped me articulate the truths behind this book. Thank you to Hal White and Hayden Wreyford on the Blueprint for Life team, whose efforts and contributions have made this book possible.

The Fulfillment Factor
©2012 Blueprint for Life, Inc.

ALL RIGHTS RESERVED

No part of this publication may be reproduced, stored in a retrieval system, or transmitted in any form, by any means–electronic, mechanical, photo-copying, recording, or otherwise–without prior written permission.

First hardcover edition, February 2013

Printed in the United States.

10 9 8 7 6 5 4 3 2 1

Cover design by Design Industry
Layout design by Hayden Wreyford

For more information:
info@blueprintforlife.com
www.blueprintforlife.com

CONTENTS

"I no longer consider my life as dear unto myself; only that I fulfill the mission and calling given to me by God himself."

Acts 20:24

Chapter One

The Fulfillment Factor

It Will Bring You Satisfaction and Joy

Most people dream of the day when they can stop working. They imagine sitting by a swimming pool sipping lemonade, golfing whenever they want, and sleeping late seven days a week. When I was 31 years old, that dream became my reality—and I was thrilled. What could be better? No more bosses. No more alarm clocks. No more *work*.

More importantly, as a dedicated follower of Christ, I believed that God had financially blessed me so I could serve Him in full-time ministry. So I began to spend a substantial amount of time every week volunteering for worthy causes. I served at a large church in Atlanta as a cameraman. I volunteered at a nationwide pro-life organization with its mission to save unborn children, and I feverishly helped a national political organization to elect Christian candidates to office. And sometimes I even sat by the pool.

But after six months, the American dream proved unfulfilling. Something was terribly wrong. Instead of experiencing a great deal of happiness and fulfillment, I was completely miserable. I assumed that having more free time, managing my own schedule, and being financially independent would cause my happiness quotient to soar off the charts.

But it didn't.

After 12 long months of dreading each day, I decided to go back into business. I obtained my license as a registered investment advisor, and became an investment banker. Thankfully, my anxiety disappeared and was replaced with passion. I was so thrilled about doing business again that I didn't even mind waking up at 3 or 4 AM so I could talk with overseas European investors. That decision to reengage in business turned out to be one of the best decisions I ever made.

Don't get me wrong. I love Christ, and He is the reason for everything I do, which is why I couldn't understand why I was so miserable in ministry but felt fulfilled and alive in business. When I discovered the answers to that question, I learned a set of truths that anyone can leverage to experience fulfillment.

I discovered that I wasn't fulfilled by serving in full-time Christian ministry because it was not the mission for which God created me. He made me to be a business man. Ministry didn't maximize my skills, talents, or passions. So I was miserable, even though I was a believer in Christ.

Maybe this describes you. Maybe you are dissatisfied even though you know Jesus. Maybe you have spent a lot of time wondering, "Why am I here?" "What's my personal mission?" "What does God want me to do with my life?" or "I am a Christian so why do I still feel unfulfilled?" If you have ever asked these questions, this book is for you. It has been written to help you discover, develop, and pursue your God-given mission so that you too can experience what I call *The Fulfillment Factor*.

To unlock the truths I discovered about fulfillment, first you need to understand why you have been created. This has been revealed in God's Master Plan. Let's discover this plan by taking a trip through the stars.

Chapter Two

God's Master Plan

It's the Reason You Are Here

Imagine that you have been chosen to take a special trip with NASA to never-visited stars and galaxies. After you endure astronaut training, you suit up, then blast off traveling the speed of light toward the star Alpha Centauri. This star is four and a half light years away, or about 250,000 times the distance to the sun.

When you reach Alpha Centauri, you think about the birthday cake you are going to eat when you get back home because four and a half years have passed. You could have traveled to the moon in one and a half seconds, or the sun in eight and a half minutes, but the Alpha trip sounded more exciting.

After stopping by Alpha Centauri, you zip through the Andromeda Galaxy, which is more than 1.5 million light years away. On the way there, you surf the Internet and learn that distant galaxies, which are visible through telescopes, are 6,500 million light years away! You also learn that the sun is so large that one million spheres of the earth could fit inside it if it were hollow—but it's not the biggest star. You discover that some stars are so large that 500 million spheres of the sun could fit inside each one if they were hollow!

But your favorite star is Betelgeuse (pronounced "Beetle Juice")—and you can't wait to see it. It is 520 light years from the earth and it's one of the brightest stars of Orion's Belt. Its diameter is 500 million kilometers, which means that if it were hollow, the earth could comfortably revolve around the sun, *inside Betelgeuse*, in its normal orbit! After stopping by Betelgeuse, you step back into your rocket completely amazed, and then zip toward home through the Milky Way.

On the way back to earth, you marvel at the 100 million stars in your home galaxy—and that the sun is just one of them. When you think about the wonder of creation, that there are at least 100 million galaxies in the space that telescopes can see—and many more beyond—you feel very small—and God seems very big.

IT'S ALL ABOUT HIS GLORY

If God wanted to remain silent about His existence, He wouldn't have bothered creating the stars; He wouldn't have made the Milky Way, or Betelgeuse. In fact, He wouldn't have made the majestic Rocky Mountains, the rippling oceans, or the magnificent hummingbird. If His goal was to remain quiet and anonymous, He wouldn't have created anything at all.

If God wanted to remain silent about His existence, He wouldn't have bothered creating the stars.

Instead, He spoke a smorgasbord for our senses into existence. Wonder for our eyes, beauty for our ears, fragrances for our noses—and rapture for our hearts. His creation screams about His unseen beauty; it shouts about His unseen qualities and His magnificence.

When Michelangelo painted the ceiling of the Sistine Chapel, he crafted an inner expression of his hidden person. In the same way, God's creation exhibited through the mountains, stars, and oceans, is an expression of the God we can't see.

God didn't remain anonymous because He didn't want to. Rather, He wanted to display His glory throughout the universe as His gift to man.

The Bible says, "The heavens declare the glory of God; the skies proclaim the work of his hands" (Psalm 19:1). Anything less grand would not have been a true representation of Himself—His indescribable, unfathomable, indefinable glory.

This is the first part of God's Master Plan: To display His glory.

GOD'S CROWN OF CREATION

It seems that it would have been enough for God to fulfill the first part of His Master Plan by glorifying Himself through the stars, but He didn't stop there. Instead, after He created the heavens and the earth, the Bible says that He created something even more amazing.

He scooped some dirt from the ground He had made and formed the very first man. It was a sacred moment.

Adam was a first edition. Nothing like this had been done before. God bent over the lifeless Adam and breathed into him to give man His spirit. He imparted Himself to man, as a mother is a part of a child.

A holy hush must have traveled through heaven. This was God's crown of creation. The breath of God in man, wrapped in human flesh.

In the same way that God created the universe to display His glory, God created people to display His glory, too. In Psalm 139:14 the psalmist says that he is "fearfully and wonderfully made." To be fearfully and wonderfully made means that you are beyond figuring out. You are a divine mystery of God. You are God's fingerprint and an expression of His glory.

Consider these facts about how you have been created. In the *Bread of Life Study*, it says:

> *Doctors tell us that the human brain has 30 billion nerve-cells, each operating at a potential of nearly one-tenth of a volt of electricity. Those over 35 years of age lose 1,000 of these nerve cells every day—and these cells are never replaced. Yet the main functions of the brain*

carry on till the end of life, even though there is a slight loss in the sensitivity of the five senses.

Did you know that each of our eyes has 130 million little rods for black and white vision and 7 million cones for color vision? These are connected to the brain by 300,000 nerve fibers. The human eye can receive 1.5 million messages simultaneously! To duplicate the function of one eye mechanically, it would require 250,000 television transmitters and receivers!

Now look at the heart and the blood vessels. We don't usually think of them until they give us some trouble! But that heart which God has put within our bodies beats 40 million times every year, without any lubrication and without taking a vacation. Even though you didn't realize it, your heart beat within your body 100,000 times yesterday, pumping blood through 100,000 kilometers of blood vessels from your head to your feet. Your body also produced more than 172 billion red blood cells just yesterday to replace the damaged and worn-out cells? Isn't it a miracle that you are alive today?

In every cell of your body, there is a very detailed instruction code. There are three billion letters of DNA code determining your hair color, how you laugh, the color of your eyes, and if you are short or tall in every cell of your body. Therefore, DNA is a three-billion-lettered program telling the cell to act in a certain way. It is a full instruction manual.

I hope you are amazed. Indeed, the God who made this world has no rivals.

It's clear that when God created man and the universe, His intent was to display His glory. His creation is so amazing that it cries out "To God be the glory!"

There is a second part to God's Master Plan that is even more amazing. Read on to discover how the God of the universe wants to have a personal and intimate relationship with you, His creation.

HE CAME

History is filled with great love stories. But the greatest love story of all time trumps all others. It's the story of the God who created the Milky Way and Betelgeuse coming to the earth to die for those He created even though they had rejected Him. It's a passionate love story of God pursuing people.

Have you ever wondered why He went to so much trouble, why He bothered with the horror of the cross? After all, since He is God and is obviously in charge, He could have taken an easier road. He could have demanded love from His creation. He could have made love mandatory. But He didn't. Instead, He did the unthinkable.

He willingly died.

In blood and brutality.

At the hands of people who falsely accused Him.

He was beaten.

Beyond recognition.

Mocked.

And nailed to a tree.

Between two criminals.

And even rejected by His Father.

God proved His love through action. Anything less would not have been a true expression of His heart and an incorrect representation of His love. Anyone who goes to so much trouble to prove love has one motive: To win love. True love is always proven by action and getting love in return is always the goal.

This is the second part of God's Master Plan: To have a love relationship with those He created—including you.

This is the second part of God's Master Plan: To have a love relationship with those He created—including you.

In his book *Soul Cravings*, author Erwin Raphael Mcmanus writes about a trip he took to the Middle East where he shared a story with a group of Muslims to convince them that the Almighty is pursuing them, that in the same way a mother wants relationship with her daughter, or a lover wants relationship with his beloved, God wants relationship with His creation.

"I once met a girl named Kim, and I fell in love,"
He said.

"I pursued her with my love and pursued her with my love until I felt my love had captured her heart. So I asked her to be my wife, and she said no."

I could feel their empathy, if not their pity.

"I was unrelenting and I asked her again, pursuing her with my love, and I pursued her with my love until she said yes."

There was a huge relief throughout the entire room.

I went on, "I did not send my brother, nor did I send my friend. For in the issues of love, you must go yourself.

This is the story of God: He pursues you with His love and pursues you with His love, and you perhaps have not said yes. And even if you reject His love, He pursues you ever still. It was not enough to send an angel or a prophet or any other, for issues of love, you must go yourself. And so God has come."

Ah, yes. God has come. He has come to make Himself known in the stars and in Betelgeuse and the wonder of the snowflake—and He came on the cross. And in His coming, His Master Plan has been fully revealed: to be glorified and have a relationship with His creation—including you. This is why you have been created.

Chapter Three

The Hole in Your Soul

It's Designed to Make You Long for God

Have you ever wondered why you have a longing in your soul that cannot be satisfied? No matter how you try to fill it with money, stuff, a great career, or new relationships, you still feel dissatisfied.

Be encouraged. You are not alone. If you live in China, Russia, or the United States, you know this longing. If you are Asian, American, or Swedish, it never leaves you. If you are 12, 25, 40, or 100, you are well acquainted with this ache.

God placed His Master Plan in your heart and it's designed to make you long for Him.

This longing might sometimes make you feel like you are incomplete and that God made a mistake when He knit you together in your mother's womb, but He didn't. He didn't leave anything out. Instead, He strategically placed this void inside of you as a gift. This is what I call the "hole in your soul." God placed His Master Plan in your heart and it's designed to make you long for Him.

If you don't have an intimate relationship with God and glorify Him with your life, it's impossible to experience true fulfillment.

In the last chapter, I revealed that God has a Master Plan that has two parts: 1) For Him to be glorified, and 2) For Him to have a relationship with the people He created. (See the graphic on the following pages.)

Because God wants to be glorified and also wants to have a personal relationship with you, what does this mean? Does He want you just go to church or check a little box on a tiny piece of paper indicating that you have accepted Him as Lord and Savior?

To suggest that God would go to such great lengths to prove His love by dying on a tree so that we would check an "I am saved" box without giving Him genuine acts of love and relationship in return is an insult to the One who made us.

If you don't have an intimate relationship with God *and* glorify Him with your life, it's impossible to experience true fulfillment.

INTIMACY WITH GOD

Joe and Judy live in the same house. They are married and share a bed. They move silently past each other each morning in the hall and brush their teeth over the same sink—but they never exchange any communication. They are strangers sharing square footage.

So it is with some people who attend church. Every Sunday they come into God's house. They hear *about* Him, but they never *hear* Him. They speak *of* Him, but they never speak *to* Him. Their "relationship" with God isn't genuine, which grieves the One who died to prove His love.

God doesn't want you to know about Him; He wants you to know Him.

To have a genuine relationship with Christ means that you communicate with Him. You tell others about Him because you are proud of Him. You think about how you can please Him, and you demonstrate your love, just as a man who loves his wife demonstrates his. God wants you to discover what's important to Him by reading the Bible, which is His love letter to you. He wants you to talk with Him and allow Him to speak to you through Scripture and the Holy Spirit. He wants you to share your ongoing life story with Him. This is the context in which intimacy grows.

Intimacy isn't just for earthly relationships; it's also for relationship with God. Some people believe that because they can't see God they can't have a real relationship with Him. You may not be able to see Him, but you can

God's Master Plan

have an intimate, vibrant relationship with Him that is as real as one with your best friend.

In the early morning hours, I spend time reading my Bible and I turn my attention toward God. I pray for Him to speak to me through His Word—and during this time I am often reminded why I have been created.

I have been created to be a businessman, husband, father, and friend. But more than anything, I have been created to be God's child. There are times when I sit with Him that a deep satisfaction swells over me. *Yes, this is what I was created for. This is where I belong.* There is nothing this side of heaven like knowing the One who knows me through and through.

Because God desires a relationship with you, He doesn't want the leftovers of your life.

I can find a lot of happiness in this world, but there is nothing that rivals the intimacy I have with my Creator. Without a relationship with Christ, nothing else in life would make sense. My personal mission would be a complete waste of time without knowing Him; He is the foundation for all that I do.

In Philippians 3:8 Paul wrote, "I consider everything a loss compared to the surpassing greatness of knowing Christ Jesus my Lord, for whose sake I have lost all things." God wants this to be true of you and me as well. To understand this is to begin to understand how to experience the greatest fulfillment and joy you can.

I want to add something very important: Because God desires a relationship with you, He doesn't want the leftovers of your life. He doesn't want your leftover affections and loyalties after you give your time and energy to your friends, finances, boss, job, children, mate, school, government, television, Twitter, or Facebook. Relationship and commitment to Christ cannot be Jesus and money, Jesus and sex, Jesus and my BMW, Jesus and my career. He wants to be your top priority.

In America, we've gotten used to mixing relationship with Christ with other affections that rival Him and we think it's okay. The result has been a watered-down version of what Jesus intended when He said, "Come, follow me."

Here's a secret: You can sense God's love. You can go to church, raise your hands, and soak in hour after hour of Christian music. You can read your Bible and memorize scriptures and still feel unfulfilled because true love is proven by action. The point of our lives must be to make Him famous, or to glorify Him. This matches His Master Plan.

GLORIFY GOD

There once was a king who wanted to make his name great among his people, so he built a grand castle with ornate spires shooting into the sky to grace his world-renowned city. The result was just what he wanted. Men worshipped him and came from near and far to see his castle and his kingdom.

Time passed and the first king died and a second king took his place. The second king wanted to make his name great as well, but he desired to build something more grand and amazing than his predecessor. So he added onto what the first king had made and erected his new addition right next to the first king's construction to grace the kingdom.

Unfortunately, the second king did not have enough money to make his structure bigger, so he made it *look* bigger by using an optical illusion. In the same way that an artist makes an object look farther away by drawing it smaller and higher on a page, the king built the windows smaller as they went higher into the sky. As a result, the building *appeared* to be taller next to the first king's construction, while in reality, it was shorter.

A lot of people in this world will go to any measure to build their own kingdom, instead of building Christ's. They will do anything to draw attention to themselves and make their name great because they think that this is going to bring them fulfillment.

However, if you want to experience the highest level of fulfillment, you must first know the God who made you. You must also make it your goal to make Him famous, which means you glorify Him.

If you want to experience the highest level of fulfillment, you must first know the God who made you. You must also make it your goal to make Him famous, which means you glorify Him.

To glorify Him means that you put the spotlight on Him and you leverage everything you can in your life to lift Him up so others can see Him. You maximize all that you have been given to show and tell others about Him. You use your money, skills, talents, and passions. You use everything that you are. If you make this your goal, you will experience a deep joy that cannot in any way come from selfishly serving yourself and building your own kingdom.

Unfortunately, our self-centered American culture has taught us that the ultimate goal is to make ourselves happy. Some people in the American church have bought into the "I-have-to-be-happy" lie—and believe that the main message of Christianity is all about them, when it's really all about God.

In his book *Radical*, David Platt writes:

> If you were to ask the average Christian sitting in a worship service on Sunday morning to summarize the message of Christianity, you would most likely hear something along the lines of "The message of Christianity is that God loves me." Or someone might say "The message of Christianity is that God loves me enough to send his Son, Jesus, to die for me."
>
> As wonderful as this sentiment sounds, is it biblical? Isn't it incomplete, based on what I have seen in the Bible? "God loves me" is not the essence of biblical Christianity. Because if

"God loves me" is the message of Christianity, then who is the object of Christianity?

God loves me.

Me.

Christianity's object is me.

Therefore, when I look for a church, I look for the music that best fits me and the programs that cater to me and my family. When I make plans for my life and career, it is about what works best for me and my family. When I consider the house I will live in, the car I will drive, the clothes I will wear, the way I live, I will choose according to what is best for me. This is the version of Christianity that largely prevails in our culture.

But it is not biblical Christianity.

The message of biblical Christianity is not "God loves me, period" as if we were the object of our own faith. The message of biblical Christianity is "God loves me so that I might make him—his ways, his salvation, his glory, and his greatness—known among all nations." Now God is the object of our faith, and Christianity centers around him. We are not the end of the gospel; God is.

You might be asking, "What about my happiness? You are telling me that God wants me to glorify Him and make Him famous. If I do what you are telling me to do, doesn't that mean that I will miss out on being happy? Doesn't God want me to be happy?"

Oh, God wants to give you more than happiness; He wants to give you joy. Happiness is fickle. It stays around only when times are feel-good. Joy is a much more faithful companion. It transcends difficulties and hardship. Joy is constant.

A man once heard that Christians were being persecuted and beaten overseas in China, he went to the CEO of a U.S.-based missions organization and said, "Someone has to stop this. It just *has* to stop."

"Really?" the man responded. "You need to come with me to China."

The man reluctantly boarded a plane. Once he arrived, he gathered with a group of Chinese Christians in a small, underground church. Several of them had just been arrested for sharing the gospel and were still being held in custody. A second group had just returned after being beaten for the same reason. All the church members were on their faces praising God, thanking Him that they had the privilege of making Him famous.

There is one very special way that you can love and glorify God like no one else can, a way that is unique to you and is a key ingredient to The Fulfillment Factor.

These Chinese Christians discovered what so many of us in the United States who seek our own glory do not know: When you give all that you are and all that you have to glorify God, then joy increases and you experience a fulfillment that is not of this world.

There is something enthralling about knowing that you aren't living as a part of the status quo. It's exhilarating when God asks you to glorify Him, and you answer the call. It's exhilarating because you know that you are taking part in something big, something unimaginably magnificent, and something eternal. You are taking part in God's everlasting kingdom!

Know this: God wants to give you full joy when you play your part in His Master Plan by intimately knowing Him and glorifying Him with your life. And, there is one very special way that you can love and glorify God like no one else can, a way that is unique to you and is a key ingredient to *The Fulfillment Factor*. Read on and I will explain.

Chapter Four

Your Personal Mission from God

Pursuing it is "The Fulfillment Factor"

As little children we believe we are designed for a unique mission. Why else would you strap on a cape and jump off your parents' roof? What else would make you believe you can save every kitten in the neighborhood by setting up a cardboard booth on the street corner and find new feline owners? When we are small, we believe we can accomplish something great because it's innate.

God made us for a mission.

This really shouldn't be a surprise because we have in us the breath of the God who made the moon, the

God created you to complete a mission for Him.

stars, Betelgeuse, and kittens—and like Him we have the desire to create and accomplish.

God created you to complete a mission for Him. He made you to do something for Him.

Here are seven principles that you'll need to know to successfully accomplish your personal, God-given mission.

Principle 1: You have a personal mission and you have been perfectly equipped for it.

Maybe you are thinking, *That sounds great, Mike, but I don't think God has a personal mission for me.* Maybe you have heard people say that they are "called" to a particular mission and you have wondered, *What am I "called" to do?*

In the upcoming chapters, we will discuss how you can recognize and embark upon your personal, unique, God-given mission. But for now, let's take a look at one of God's smallest creatures for an inspiring reminder that we have all been made for mission.

Every day outside the entrance of my office building, a flurry of bees bop from one colorful flower to another to forage for nectar. According to blogger Tony Fuentes, "When a bee visits a flower. . . some of the flower's pollen rubs off on the bee's. . . fuzzy, little belly. The bee then moves on to another flower and some of the pollen on his belly is transferred to that flower. Without this simple act of pollination, plants wouldn't give birth to seeds or fruit. Crops would fail and farmers would go bankrupt."

It's incredible that God has given even the little bee a job to do. Tony adds the amazing fact that approximately every three mouthfuls of food we enjoy is the direct result of pollination done by our "fuzzy, black and yellow, jumpsuit-wearing friends."

Doesn't it make logical sense that because God has a job for the tiny bee that He has a mission for you, the crown of His creation?

Let me ask you: Doesn't it make logical sense that because God has a job for the tiny bee that He has a mission for you, the crown of His creation?

Ephesians 2:10 says, "For we are God's workmanship, created in Christ Jesus to do good works, which God prepared in advance for us to do." *Prepared in advance.* Before God spoke the Milky Way into existence, before Betelgeuse, before the earth was placed on its axis, God planned you and He prepared you to do good works which support His Master Plan.

Friend, before the foundation of the world, you were designed by Him and for Him. You have a mission.

Principle 2: Your mission must help fulfill God's purposes in the world.

Throughout Scripture, Jesus has commanded us to evangelize—or tell others about Him—such as in Mark 16:15 which says, "Go into all the world and preach the good news to all creation." There are also numerous scriptures which show that we are to care for the poor and needy, such as 1 Timothy 5:3, which indicates that we are to care for widows. Jesus has also said that we should teach others how to follow Him. This is called "discipleship." These are three main purposes God wants to accomplish in the world.

God's purposes in the world are evangelism, discipleship, and caring for the poor and needy.

Tom Turco is from Boise, Idaho. Each summer, for over thirteen years Tom has worked as a director for Royal Family Kids' Camp, an international organization dedicated to ministering to abused and neglected children. Tom's 9-5 job is as an electrical engineer, but his God-given mission is to show Jesus' love to underprivileged kids each summer at RFKC in the Idaho mountains.

Every June, kids who have been referred to RFKC through Health and Welfare load onto a bus and arrive at camp with hugs, hollers, and cheers from the camp staff.

Sarah, a 6-year-old who bounced in and out of 14 foster homes in 12 months finally understood RFKC's goal after her third year at camp. "It's about love," she said. Indeed it is. Because many of the campers come from low-income families, birthday gifts are a privilege that many can't afford, so each child receives a box of birthday surprises.

Tom says, "I never realized how some kids have never had something like the items that we see in dollar stores, like pencils and barrettes. Some of them get so excited. This year, one 7-year-old boy yelled, 'Look at what God gave me!' We've had foster parents say, 'This is the best thing that happens to these kids all year.' Some of them even start packing for camp in January."

Through RFKC, Tom is pursuing his personal mission to help fulfill God's purposes in world. Your mission may be to finance groups that evangelize, write discipleship materials, or you may start an organization that uses the Internet to spread God's Word to millions. Whatever your personal mission, it needs to help accomplish God's purposes in the world.

Principle 3: Your mission may be the same—or different—than your career.

After my stint in ministry and by the pool, I met Eric Swartz who became my partner in our new investment banking firm. On the first day we opened our doors, Eric and I decided to develop a giving fund. We made a commitment to give the first 10 cents of every dollar we earned in revenue to a charitable cause or ministry in need. We also started a non-profit called Ministry Ventures. Since its beginning in 1999, Ministry Ventures has launched over 60 faith-based organizations that support God's work all over the world.

True fulfillment comes from using your gifts and talents for something much bigger than yourself.

Through my career as an investment banker, I am helping God fulfill His purposes in the world, which is why I am so passionate about my career. If I was using my gifts and talents only to make money, I would be unsatisfied and miserable. True fulfillment doesn't come from just using one's gifts and talents. True fulfillment comes from using your gifts and talents for something much bigger than yourself.

God has created some men to be cameramen, some to work as advocates for pro-life organizations, and some to be missionaries and pastors. But as I mentioned, He created me to be a businessman. Because this is how I have been designed, this is how I can best glorify Him to experience maximum fulfillment and joy in my life.

Unlike me, perhaps your career and God-given mission are identical. For example, maybe you are a pastor so your career and mission are the same. Or maybe your story is more like mine. Perhaps your career *supports* your God-given mission, which it always should.

Tragically, a lot of people make the error of sacrificing their personal mission on the altar of their career. They live for this present world and for what their career can give them, such as more money, comfort,

Remember that your career or job must always support—and never hinder—your mission to fulfill God's purposes in the world.

41

or status. As a result, their career hinders their God-given mission, and the people who God could touch through them become spiritual casualties of selfishness. Remember that your career or job must always support—and never hinder—your mission to help fulfill God's purposes in the world.

Principle 4: God won't waste a thing in your mission.

You might be saying, "I have so much against me. I can't pursue my personal mission. I grew up in a horrible family." "I was abused." "I don't have any money." "I am single." "I am divorced." Or, "I am too young." There are many reasons why we can each feel that we can't pursue our mission.

Be encouraged. God doesn't waste a thing. Your inadequacies and your history will both be leveraged by God as powerful components that will work in your favor to complete your mission.

Who better to work with abused children than someone who has been abused? Who could be more powerful in helping the poor and needy than one who has been poor and needy? Who can provide better comfort for the grieving than the one who has grieved? God will weave your history and even the things that you consider to be inadequacies into your mission.

In 2 Corinthians 12:1-4, the apostle Paul writes about some special revelations that God gave him of heaven in which "he was caught up to paradise and heard inexpressible things, things that no one is permitted to tell." Then in verse 7, he writes, "Therefore, in order to keep me from becoming conceited because of these surpassingly great revelations, there was given me a thorn in my flesh, a messenger of Satan, to torment me."

There are different ideas about what his ailment was. But no matter what it was, God used this "thorn in the flesh" to keep Paul humble so that he could more effectively complete his mission. Even in Paul's life, God used what could have been a hindrance as a positive part of Paul's mission.

Principle 5: Your mission is a part of God's mosaic.

Every day the bees outside my office bop from one flower to the next, doing what God has naturally designed them to do. They have no idea that their pollinating skills are impacting a local farmer, or that a little boy sitting at the dinner table somewhere across the country has food to

43

eat because of their talent. They are clueless that they fit into a larger picture of creation.

In the same way that the bee is a part of God's bigger picture, you are too. Every person God has created fits into what I call "God's mosaic." You are a small piece of this mosaic, which consists of millions of people in the world today. God is calling you to be active in His mosaic by doing what only you can do through your mission, using your unique God-given passions, skills and talents to fulfill His purposes in the world.

Principle 6: Don't just sit in the driveway.

When I was 14 years old, I landed my first big job as a paper boy for the *Daily Ledger* in Enterprise, Alabama. I still remember the elation and thrill I experienced when I received $50 after working for one month. Getting up at 4:00 AM on Sunday morning to deliver papers, sometimes in the cold and rain, seemed a small price to pay for such a lucrative sum.

Having a relationship with Jesus without fulfilling your personal mission is like filling up your car with gas and letting it sit in the driveway.

Little did I know at the time that such hard work would lay the groundwork to purchase, at age 16, my first car. It was a silver Pontiac Firebird with an orange stripe down the side. After the salesman handed me the keys and I drove it off the lot, the first thing I did was fill up the gas tank. Then I took it out for a long drive. It was summer, so I rolled down the windows, cranked up the stereo, and went on a driving adventure because that is what you do when you are 16 years old and you get some new wheels.

Having a relationship with Jesus without fulfilling your personal mission is like filling up your car with gas and letting it sit in the driveway. You'll miss out on adventure with God, expressing your love to Him through action, and you will also miss out on the fulfillment that only partnering with Him can bring.

In John 10:10, Jesus said, "I have come that they [that's you and me] may have life, and have it to the full." God wants to bless you with a full, joy-filled life when you participate in His Master Plan by pursuing your personal mission. The next principle is a dire warning for people who know Christ as our Savior but because of fear, doubt,

The next principle is a dire warning for people who know Christ as our Savior but because of fear, doubt, or selfishness, fail to pursue their personal mission from God.

or selfishness, fail to pursue their personal mission from God.

Principle 7: There are three trade-offs for not accomplishing your personal mission.

You will sacrifice joy for happiness.   Maybe it doesn't sound bad to trade joy for happiness, but happiness isn't consistent. It comes and goes. You can experience it only when things are going good—and even then, it doesn't stick around. As soon as the initial excitement wears off, you'll need another shot of something good to bring happiness back. It's not fulfilling in the long run.

Thankfully, the joy that comes from pursuing your personal mission doesn't work that way. The joy God gives isn't dampened by gloomy weather or a bad economy, and it doesn't fade after the novelty is gone. It transcends life's circumstances. Joy is rooted in a deep sense of knowing who you belong to and that you are walking in His will. When you participate in God's Master Plan by

If you claim to know God but don't engage in what He's prepared you to do, then you'll never have a fully developed relationship with Him.

46

knowing Him and fulfilling your personal mission, you will find there is no greater joy.

You will sacrifice full relationship with God for doing things your own way. Again, maybe that doesn't sound like a bad trade, but knowing God and doing His will are inseparable concepts. If you claim to know God but don't engage in what He's prepared you to do, then you'll never have a fully developed relationship with Him.

You will trade eternal rewards for temporary amusement. The word *amusement* comes from the Latin word *muse*, which means "to think," and the prefix *a*, which means "not." When our goal is temporary amusement, we're just not thinking. Admittedly, sometimes it can feel good not to think. But it's like using a credit card. It will cost you more later. When it comes to God's mission for your life, and especially how your mission will affect others, that's a high price to pay.

You are an eternal being. You will live forever, either in paradise with your heavenly Father or in darkness separated from God. Your salvation depends on placing your faith in Christ as your Redeemer and Savior.

But the Bible also says that you will be rewarded in heaven based on how well you do His will in the world. What we do now with our opportunities, skills, talents, and treasures will determine the rewards we receive for eternity. This is a very big deal that we will talk more about in the last chapter of this book.

I hope that you are getting excited. If you aren't, you should be. Here's why:

1) God, the Creator of the Universe, wants an intimate relationship with you.

2) He has specifically designed and equipped you for a mission to glorify Him. As a result you can experience a life of joy and fulfillment.

Chapter Five

Discovering Your Personal Mission from God

The Life Impact Triangle Points to Your Personal Mission

Ever since I was a kid I had a nagging fear of normalcy. Maybe it was because I grew up on a farm outside a very normal, small southern town of Enterprise, Alabama. Maybe it was because my parents worked 9 to 5 for the government throughout their careers. Maybe it was because I was just a very ordinary kid. I was not the best student, not very athletic, and not even a mention in the high school yearbook.

After high school I signed up for the Aerospace Engineering program at Auburn University. I chose aerospace engineering because I'd always enjoyed math, and I figured rockets were the fastest way to get wherever I was going.

With my aerospace engineering degree in hand, I quickly landed a job with Pratt & Whitney Aircraft in West Palm Beach, Florida. Imagine the response when I told people that my new job was developing the most advanced military aircraft in the world.

My fear of being ordinary made itself obvious on my very first day on the job. I wouldn't say the division where I reported was a cubicle farm, but something about it reeked of predictability. In my mind, it represented the kind of normalcy I had vowed to escape.

As I looked across the office where I worked, I could practically mark out the years in cubicles. My cube represented year one—entry level. Eleven feet away, my boss's cube represented the 20-year mark. And 17 feet beyond that, my boss's boss sat at the 30-year mark.

The Life Impact Triangle points you toward your God-given mission so that you can make a big impact with your life.

The rest of my life was to be a 28-foot journey from a small cubicle to a medium one to a large one. No matter how hard I worked, or how much I accomplished, I would never go any farther in life than 28 feet. It felt almost morbid. And it was more than I could bear.

My guess is that like me, you don't want to be ordinary either. Instead, you want to pursue an extraordinary, joy-filled life in which your life makes a big impact. To do that, and to begin to discover your personal mission from God, I'd like to introduce you to the Life Impact Triangle.

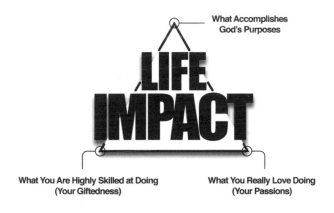

What Accomplishes
God's Purposes

LIFE IMPACT

What You Are Highly Skilled at Doing
(Your Giftedness)

What You Really Love Doing
(Your Passions)

The Life Impact Triangle points you toward your God-given mission so that you can make a big impact with your life. Notice it has three points:

1) What you really love doing (your passions)

2) Your skills and talents (or giftedness) and

3) God's purposes for the world.

When all three points intersect, the result will be a big impact for God's kingdom and in the lives of others—and that's no ordinary life.

To understand this special triangle and how to make it a reality in your life, let's first take a look at your passions.

WHAT DO YOU LOVE TO DO (YOUR PASSIONS)?

During a long weekend when my wife and kids are out of town, I always end up in the same place: downstairs on the computer evaluating publicly traded companies and the stock market. For some people this would feel like torture, but for me, it's an absolute joy.

There is something about seeking out the best performing companies in the world and finding those hidden values in the market that exhilarates me. I may start looking at the market at 5:00 PM and the next thing I know it's 12:00 AM. Time passes quickly because studying the stock market is one of my passions.

The first point of the Life Impact Triangle focuses on what you really love doing, or your passions. Your passions are your first clue to help you define your personal mission from God. To understand how you fit into this point of the triangle, ask yourself these questions:

» What do I really enjoy?

» What kind of work do I find rewarding?

» What do I gravitate toward when I have some extra time?

» What activities am I doing when time flies by?

Sparky Anderson, the legendary baseball manager, once said, "I can't believe they pay us to play baseball—something we did for free as kids." Anderson's comment revealed that when you have a passion for something, it's a great motivator, which is why it's important to understand what you love to do.

When you know what you love to do, you'll know what you are passionate about, which means

When you know what you love to do, you'll know what you are passionate about, which means you'll tap into energy to fuel your God-given mission.

you'll tap into energy to fuel your God-given mission. Without passion, it's difficult to do anything with much endurance—and endurance is definitely needed for any God-sized mission.

Maybe you are thinking, *Well, I'm not passionate.* Be encouraged. Everyone has a passion for something. You were born with it. Maybe you don't have a passionate personality, but you still have passion. Particular things interest you more than others. These are your passions.

If you are having a difficult time identifying your passions, here are some additional questions:

» Are you interested in politics?

» Do you long to cure diseases which inflict suffering on children?

» Do you have a special concern to see justice served?

» Do you lie awake at night over the thought that people are starving halfway around the world?

» Are you moved by excellent communication?

» Do you like leading other people, or are you a follower?

» Do you enjoy fixing problems, or would you rather come into the picture once everything is running smoothly?

» As you think back over your life, when has your sense of passion felt the strongest? What were you doing in those situations? And what was it about them that could be identified as passion?

What Are You Skilled At Doing?

In his book *The Element*, Sir Ken Robinson tells a story about a 6-year-old boy named Bart who loved to walk on his hands. No one knew why, but it was so easy for him that people said he could walk as easily on his hands as on his feet.

His classmates often asked him to demonstrate his trick, and each time he happily popped into a handstand and began walking around on his hands. Eventually Bart could even walk up and down the stairs on his hands—and he loved it.

One day, Bart's physical education teacher got permission from his parents to take him on a field trip to a fully-equipped training center for gymnastics. As he walked in, Bart was amazed.

In the book, Sir Ken Robinson writes,

> *He'd never seen anything so wondrous in his life. There were ropes, parallel bars, trapezes, ladders, trampolines, hurdles—all kinds of things upon which he could climb, cavort, and swing. It was like visiting Santa's workshop and Disneyland at the same time. It was the ideal place for him. His life turned in that moment. Suddenly his innate skills were good for something more than amusing himself and others.*

In the years that followed, Bart Conner trained hard and in 1976 he became a household name in the Montreal Olympics as a gymnast for the United States. He also represented the United States in 1980 and 1984. Bart became the most decorated male American gymnast in history, and was inducted into every major Hall of Fame for his sport.

Maybe it seems like a huge disconnect between gymnastics and God's purposes of evangelism, discipleship, and caring for the poor and needy. However, as I mentioned in Chapter Four, your career and your mission may not be the same, but any career can be leveraged to fulfill God's purposes in the world and bring Him glory. A first step is identifying what you love to do.

I recently heard a story of a professional golfer who leverages his time on the green as an evangelist to fulfill God's purposes in the world. He strategically writes scriptures on his golf balls so that when other golfers retrieve them, they often notice the scripture and make a comment. This provides him with an open door to talk about His Lord. He has turned golf into an evangelism tool. Not only is this man doing what he loves to do, he is combining it with His love for His Savior. In this there is no greater fulfillment.

Can you imagine what even greater things this man could do for God if he taught other golfers to do the same? What if he started a nationwide club for golfers interested in evangelism? God can use every passion, every talent, and every skill for His kingdom. He won't waste a thing if we will give Him everything.

Here are some good questions to get you thinking about your skills and talents:

Are you. . .

> » Athletic?

> » Analytical?

> » A strategic thinker?

> » Good at building things?

> » Skilled in math and science?

> » Strong in language and verbal skills?

> » Are you a "big-picture" person or do you like project details?

> » Are you an articulate speaker?

> » Can you make people laugh?

> » Do you play a musical instrument well?

> » Can you paint?

> » Do you like large crowds or small groups?

> » Do you prefer to network at a large party or would you prefer to have a personal conversation in a coffee shop?

» What can you do well with little effort that others have to struggle or expend large amounts of energy to do?

» Do your friends call on you in times of trouble to provide insight?

» Do people seek you out to have fun?

» To talk?

» To make a business decision?

» To grieve over the loss of a loved one?

» To help them with their kids?

» At what times do people want your involvement?

These questions can help point you toward your God-given mission.

Maybe you feel like you are relatively good at many things, but not really skilled at anything. If this is how you feel, take a first look at your passions. Sometimes before our skills are developed, passion will be the only thing pointing to personal mission. In fact, it's even possible to not be aware that you are good at something until you step out and exercise that skill. For this reason, let me encourage you. Skills are like little seeds. Like a plant, they have to be "watered" to grow—and you water them by using them.

This is where courage comes in. Some people refuse to risk because it is uncomfortable. I think this is where many, many people miss their mission. God has planted a little seed inside of them so He calls them out: "Psssst, child. I want you to preach for me." But because they allow fear to come in, they decide they can't do it before they have even tried.

If you want to fulfill your mission, if you want to experience fulfillment, then you have to take risks in the early stages of using your skills.

When you combine your skills and passions with God's power to fulfill His purposes in the world, you can experience great fulfillment—and that's no ordinary life.

Be bold in pursuing all points of the Life Impact Triangle. When you combine your skills and passions with God's power to fulfill His purposes in the world, you can experience great fulfillment—and that's no ordinary life.

Chapter Six

Your Mission May Not Be What You Think

God's Ways Are Not Our Ways

I like movies when the good guy accomplishes his mission. For example, in *The Lord of the Rings*, Frodo miraculously succeeds in destroying the Ring. In *Apollo 13*, a mission gone awry is completed with a daring and thrilling journey back to the safety of earth. And in the movie *Rudy*, Rudy overcomes multiple obstacles to fulfill his dream to play football for the University of Notre Dame. I like these films because I love it when a mission is accomplished in glory.

When I think about a mission of glory, could there be anything more absurd than the cross? Nothing seems more "anti-glory" than God coming to earth to save His creation from sin by allowing Himself to be murdered. It's definitely not how we would have written God's script. If it was up to us, we'd craft His story like a Hollywood movie. We'd blow up the bad guys, shoot lightning from heaven, and descend in a cloud of fire.

Even the Jews would have rewritten Jesus' script. They expected a Warrior-Messiah coming to save them from their oppressors. But that is not how Christ served up salvation on His mission. He did it much differently—and we shouldn't be surprised. After all, Isaiah 55:8 says, "My ways are not your ways and my thoughts are not your thoughts."

Because Jesus' mission was accomplished in an unlikely way, it makes sense that our personal missions will be accomplished using unlikely methods, too.

According to Isaiah, Christ's mission was consistent with God's character of being upside-down from the world's way of thinking. Therefore, because Jesus' mission was accomplished in an unlikely way, it makes sense that our personal missions will be accomplished using unlikely methods, too. God may ask you to use your skills, talents, and passions in ways and situations that you wouldn't expect.

Take John the Baptist for example. He was Jesus' public relations guy. The Bible says that God assigned him the specific mission to put the spotlight on Christ (John 1:6-8). Because this is what he was created for, he did it very well. One day when he saw Jesus coming, he proclaimed, "Look, [everybody!] the Lamb of God, who takes away the sin of the world!" (John 1:29).

Being the PR guy for God sounds like an awesome assignment, but if you have read all of John's story, you know that God reserves the right to use us on our mission how He chooses.

After John the Baptist spent three years pointing others to Christ, John was arrested, thrown into prison, and beheaded. To the natural mind this seems unfair. But remember, your mission is all about Him. You are the clay, He is the potter (Isaiah 64:8). You have been bought with a price (1 Corinthians 6:20). Jesus said that a servant is not greater than his master (John 15:20). He has the right to use your skills, talents, and passions for your mission in a way that doesn't make sense.

Don't get me wrong, I am not saying that you will be martyred, although Christians around the world die every day for their faith. I am saying that your mission, in many ways, may not be what you think.

Here are three additional ways that your mission may not play out the way you anticipate.

His Ways Are Opposite Of The World's Ways

When you begin your personal mission to fulfill God's purposes in the world, it's important to keep His ways in mind, which, as we already discovered, are different than the world's ways. For example:

The world says, "Be the top dog! The one who is worshipped wins."

But God's Word says, "If you want to be great in my kingdom, you have to be a servant of all" (Mark 9:35).

The world says, "Repay those who hurt you."

God's Word says, "Do not repay evil for evil" (Romans 12:17).

The world says, "Look out for no. 1."

God's Word says, "If anyone would come after me, he must deny himself and take up his cross daily and follow me" (Luke 9:23).

The world says, "Get all you can and keep everything for yourself."

God's Word says, "Give to the one who asks you, and do not turn away from the one who wants to borrow from you" (Matthew 5:42).

The world says, "Make friends with influential people for self-promotion."

God's Word says, "Do nothing out of selfish ambition or vain conceit, but in humility consider others better than yourselves. Each of you should not only look to your own interests, but also to the interests of others" (Philippians 2:3-4).

The world says, "The one who dies with the most toys wins."

God's Word says, "Watch out! Be on guard against all kinds of greed; a man's life does not consist in the abundance of his possessions" (Luke 12:15).

The world says, "It's all about me."

God's Word says, "It's all about Me."

If you want to accomplish your personal mission from God and experience fulfillment, you must go against the world's ways. There will be times when following God in your mission will be uncomfortable and unpopular. People may not understand you, just as they didn't understand Jesus. But when you obey Him and leverage all that you have and are for Him, you can go to bed each night with a deep joy that no one can take away. You will be aligned with the heart of your Creator.

> *If you want to accomplish your personal mission from God and experience fulfillment, you must go against the world's ways.*

YOUR MISSION WILL BE BIGGER THAN YOU

In the last chapter I told you that you are perfectly equipped for your personal mission, and indeed you are. God has given you passion, skills, and talent, but at times you will *feel* totally unequipped. There will be moments or seasons when you will feel stretched; your mission will be "bigger than you."

Sometimes your mission will be bigger than you because you have a larger-than-life dream that God has placed in your heart, and you know you can't complete it without Him. Other times, He may strategically thrust you into a mission to glorify Him and you know you will fail without His help. Either way, the mission won't be easily achieved.

When God called Joshua to a "marching mission" to make the walls of Jericho fall down, there was no way that he could accomplish this mission in his own strength. Joshua used his gifts and talents but he was stretched far beyond his own strength and resources because he needed God's power to experience "mission accomplished." This is why God was glorified when the walls came tumbling down. Joshua couldn't take credit.

When God put it in Nehemiah's heart to rebuild the wall of Jerusalem, he didn't have the supplies he needed. He had the natural skills, talents, and passion to do the job. He was a leader, a strategist, and he was bold. But just like Joshua, Nehemiah couldn't accomplish the mission without God's help. God had to give Nehemiah favor with King Artaxerxes to accomplish the task because it was "bigger than" Nehemiah.

When God told Moses that He was sending him to speak to Pharaoh to convince him to let the Israelites go, Moses felt incapable. He said, "Oh Lord, I have never been eloquent, neither in the past nor since you have spoken to your servant. I am slow of speech and tongue" (Exodus 4:10). Moses asked God to send someone else in his place. As a result, God sent Aaron with Moses to speak for him. Even though Moses felt inadequate, it didn't stop God from using him for a mission. And just like Joshua and Nehemiah, he needed God to show up because Moses' mission was "bigger than" him.

The world tells you that you have to be in control of all aspects of your mission and you shouldn't admit a need for help. This is not God's way. Even Jesus leaned into His Father as He pressed into His mission. Psalm 147:10 says, "His pleasure is not in the strength of the horse, nor his delight in the legs of a man; the LORD delights in those who fear [revere] him, who put their hope in his unfailing love." He also says, "Not by might, nor by power, but by my Spirit says the Lord" (Zechariah 4:6).

When God wants to demonstrate His glory and make His name great, He isn't looking for the most capable person or the one who believes they are self-sufficient. He is looking for the person who is willing to use what He has placed in their hand to partner with Him to accomplish what seems impossible.

If you don't have a mission to glorify God that is bigger than you, ask Him to give you one. Say, "Lord, how can I glorify you to help fulfill your purposes in the world? Lord, use me for something bigger than me! God, stretch me! Give me your big mission for my life so that I can make you famous."

Tragically, most of us dream far too small. The only missions we have for God are the ones we can control and accomplish in our own strength with the resources we already possess. Dream big for God and remember this: What you can do in your own strength is only the beginning of how He can use you for His glory to change the lives of others. Can you imagine what He could do through you if you pursued what could only be accomplished with God as your partner?

Can you imagine what He could do through you if you pursued what could only be accomplished with God as your partner?

69

YOUR MISSION WILL TAKE YOU OUTSIDE YOUR COMFORT ZONE

I mentioned that after I graduated from college, I entered the workforce as an aerospace engineer. My parents were proud, and I was glad to have my new diploma in hand. But from the very first day at my new job I knew I was going to be miserable. Little stimulation. No creativity. Stuck in a little grey box crunching numbers. I quickly discovered that engineering wasn't for me. So after three years, and much to my parents' disappointment, I traded my secure income at my aerospace engineering job to become a copier salesman.

One day I was designing jet fighters, and the next day I was pulling a copier down the street and getting doors slammed in my face. When I called my mom and dad to tell them about my new position, they were shocked. "How could you throw five years of engineering school down the drain to sell copiers?"

I knew they wouldn't understand, but I had a deep-down feeling that I was made for something more. I knew that God had created me with other skills, talents, and passions. If I wanted to be all that He had called me to be, I had to trade what was comfortable for what was uncomfortable.

There were some drawbacks to the job. One, I was working straight commission. That meant I wasn't sure if I would get a paycheck anytime soon. Two, I had to load up a van full of copiers each morning at 8 AM in a suit and tie in muggy West Palm Beach, Florida weather. Three, each day I was required to make 50 walk-in cold calls–before lunch.

Most of my prospects kicked me out within five seconds of walking into their office. The rejection was unbearable. At the end of my first day on the job, I sat in my van and sobbed.

After the first month or two and many tears and fears behind me, I started to make some sales and actually became one of the top copier salesmen in south Florida.

As word got out to management that there was an engineering guy who could actually sell, I got a phone call from the copier company's parent company. It just so happened that the parent company was a two-billion-dollar defense contractor and was looking for engineers with sales experience to market their products to the

Pentagon. To make a long story short, I landed a job with Harris Corporation and was on my way to a successful career as a businessman.

What I didn't realize at the time is that my decision to leave my engineering job turned out to be a pivotal point in my career and central to my God-given mission. If I had never made the choice to get outside my "aerospace-engineer" box, I wouldn't be where I am today, leveraging my career to support my personal mission to financially support Christian organizations that are making Jesus famous.

Here's my big point: If you refuse to be uncomfortable in your personal mission, your mission will be limited by your current level of comfort. At every step of your mission when you want to make more impact for God, you will need faith—and that sometimes means stepping into the unknown. You can't fulfill your personal mission without risk, just as you can't fulfill it without vision.

If you refuse to be uncomfortable in your personal mission, your mission will be limited by your current level of comfort.

Chapter Seven

Developing a Vision for Your Mission

Create a Big Vision with God as Your Partner

Imagine that it's a sunny Saturday afternoon in June. You have a few free hours so you decide to go rafting a couple miles from your home. You call your best buddy and invite him to join you. Within the hour he knocks on your front door. You take him to the garage and he helps you pack what you need for your excursion: the raft, two life jackets, bottled water, sunscreen, a couple towels, and your sack lunches. After everything is loaded in your truck, your friend looks around and asks, "Where are the paddles?"

"Oh, we're not taking any," you respond. "We don't need them. We are just going to let the river take us wherever."

Your friend raises an eyebrow, stares at you, and gives you an "Are-you-crazy?" look. Everyone knows that no one goes rafting without paddles. You need them for guidance. Without them, you'll end up stuck in some trees along the river, or sucked into a current, and you'll definitely miss your destination.

It's tragic that a lot of people float the river of life without any "paddles." In this life, your paddles are your vision for your God-given mission. That vision plays a huge role in getting you where you need to go to accomplish God's purposes in the world.

Most people live without much intention so they let the river of life take them wherever it wills. As a result, they make little impact in this present world and more importantly, for eternity.

Most people live without much intention so they let the river of life take them wherever it wills. As a result, they make little impact in this present world and more importantly, for eternity.

RELY ON GOD

Remember that as you develop your vision you will need to remain flexible because your vision won't develop in a straight line. But that's okay, because it's really *His* mission and the good works He ordained for you to do before the foundation of the world (Ephesians 1:4). He has the right to change your direction anytime. Your job is to remain sensitive to His will.

In his book *Radical*, David Platt provides a great perspective on planning and vision: "Yes, we work, we plan, we organize, we create, but we do it all while we fast, while we pray, and while we confess our need for the provision of God." The person who recognizes their need for God as they plan their vision is the person who recognizes their need for God's grace—and this pleases the Father.

Here are some additional principles to keep in mind as you develop your vision to glorify Him and help accomplish His purposes in the world.

THINK BIG BUT FOCUS ON ONE STEP AT A TIME

You might be wondering, *How exactly do I develop a vision? I have an idea of my personal mission to help fulfill God's purposes in the world, but I don't know how to get there.*

The most important thing to remember is to create a big goal for your mission, but focus on one small step at a time.

At age 26 after I landed my job as a salesman for Harris Corporation, I drove a pea-green Honda Accord that had been handed down to us from my wife's aunt. It had sheepskin seat covers and was such a bomb that if Homeland Security had existed back then, it would have been confiscated it to protect the American citizens.

Every morning, I drove my pea-green Honda to Denny's, where I ordered a cup of coffee and pulled my microcassette recorder out of my briefcase. In these morning moments, every bright goal I had for my future tumbled out of my mind and through my lips to be recorded for recollection later that day in a powerful rendition of my life's future attractions.

I verbalized what I wanted to happen in my life. I said who I wanted to be and what I wanted to accomplish. "I want to be the top salesman at a national software company." "I want to own a business."

Each evening at 6:00 PM, I left work and drove home in my little car the same way I had come and listened to my morning recording. Over the next year and a half, my dreams played back to me over and over, day after day, after I drove to Denny's and recorded my desires.

Five years later, after moving to Atlanta, I was in the basement of my home where I worked to clear out an overstuffed junk closet. While sifting through a pile of papers, I came across an old shoebox filled with my dreams on microcassette.

I dusted off each cassette, refreshed the player with new batteries, and listened to one cassette, then another, then another. I couldn't believe what I was hearing. Events that I could not have manipulated into happening had become reality. Owning a business, a restaurant, in fact. Being the top software salesman in a Fortune 500 company and achieving financial success.

I was no longer driving the pea-green Honda, and I was living out my dreams—but not only my dreams. They were the dreams that God had placed in my heart. I was fulfilling His mission for my life. Some might say that because I verbalized them that they became a reality, but I believe it was more than that.

My dreams started with God. He gave them to me, and I dared to desire and believe. Then, in a way that only He can do, He connected my passions, skills, talents, and circumstances together in a magnificent result.

As you pray and ask God how you can fulfill His purposes in the world, dream big, but focus on one step at a time.

When I started recording my goals, I didn't think just about the end result; I also thought about what I would need to do to get where I wanted to go. While I knew what I wanted the end result to be, I also didn't look too far ahead. Otherwise I would have been overwhelmed. I set a big goal, but developed a vision for one small step at a time until I reached my destination.

It has to be the same for you. As you pray and ask God how you can fulfill His purposes in the world, dream big, but focus on one step at a time. He will equip you as you move along the stepping-stones to your "God-sized Vision."

YOUR VISION MUST BE DEFINED BY BELIEF

On May 6, 1954, Roger Bannister, a 25-year-old medical student, stepped into the runner's starting blocks at

Oxford's Iffley Road track outside London, England. Bannister was running against his old university for the Amateur Athletic Association.

The competition was stiff, but to everyone's surprise, Bannister defeated the other runners in his heat. He also surpassed every man in history who had competed in the mile run, because he was the first man to shatter the four-minute mile.

For years, experts thought it was humanly impossible to run a mile in less than four minutes—and decades of races had consistently proven their theory. So naturally, news of Bannister's run shocked the world.

But what happened next was even more amazing. Less than two months later, Australia's John Landy beat Bannister's world-record time with another sub-four-minute mile. That same year, New Zealand's Peter Snell joined Bannister and Landy, bettering the pace even more. And in the months that followed, dozens more runners joined the sub-four club. It was soon commonplace to break four minutes.

For centuries, four minutes had marked the limit of human achievement, and every man who stepped onto the track bowed submissively to this common preconception. But on May 6, 1954, Bannister shattered the old myth. And in the process, he issued an invitation for runners everywhere to join him.

Soon they joined him in droves. Did he introduce a new running style? A special way to train? Dietary secrets? No. Bannister simply contributed the one thing that had been missing all those years: *belief*. Once runners *saw* it done, they had no choice but to believe it *could* be done. If Bannister could do it, so could they.

Bannister's contemporaries were limited by one thing: their level of belief. They desired to break the four-minute mile, and they were clearly capable—but only when they believed it could be done did they succeed. The same principle applies to you. Your level of belief is often the only thing that holds you where you are, so your vision must include belief. Belief that God can do through you what you can't do on your own will propel you forward to accomplish your mission for God.

When you believe that with God all things are possible (Matthew 19:26), and you know that He has personally equipped and designed you for your mission, you will be encouraged to develop a belief-filled vision. God wants you to participate in His Master Plan and love and glorify Him, so it's logical that He is inviting you to have a big level of belief to do something special for Him.

Just imagine what He can do through you if you believe and say yes to God.

YOUR VISION MUST MATCH YOUR MAKEUP

When I was growing up a few people told me, "You can be anything you want to be." Because they wanted to be encouraging, they said that if I worked hard enough and believed big enough, I would succeed. I understand that I just told you that big belief will propel you toward your God-given mission. Let me clarify that: There are some things that you can't do, and if you can do them, you won't do them well because it's not how you are wired.

God wants you to participate in His Master Plan and love and glorify Him, so it's logical that He is inviting you to have a big level of belief to do something special for Him. Just imagine what He can do through you if you believe and say yes to God.

To make the biggest impact for God that you can, you need to operate within your skills, talents, and passions, and not try to be like someone else.

Do you remember the bees outside my office building that I mentioned in Chapter 4? Imagine that one of those bees thought, *I don't want to be a bee. I want to be a bird. Birds have more fun. People aren't afraid of them like they are of bees. I want to be a bird.*

Then imagine that the bee developed a vision to help him succeed in becoming a bird. As you can imagine, no matter how big the bee's vision, or how hard he concentrated, prayed, or spoke self-affirming words, he would never become a bird because a bee can be only what a bee has been designed to be.

When belief and your God-given design meet Gods' power, watch out! This is when you can make a big, big impact for God.

My point is this: While your vision needs to be supported by big belief and faith in God to help you accomplish your mission, it also must match your makeup. When belief and your God-given design meet Gods' power, watch out! This is when you can make a big, big impact for God.

Now imagine that the bee said, "I want to pollinate as many flowers as I can for God to feed as many people in the world as possible. I will pollinate more flowers than any other bee in the garden." Now *that* is something the bee could believe big about, because his vision matches his design. When you are developing your vision, always mold it around your natural skills, talents, and passions.

I am five feet nine inches tall. Imagine that I had a big desire to be a center on a pro-basketball team and I think, *This will be great. I will play professional basketball and I will start a foundation from the money I make to take care of orphans.* As much as this is a worthwhile mission, I would fail in it no matter how much I believed because God hasn't given me the height I would need to be the center for the Celtics. But my skills, talents, and passions do support being a successful businessman for Christ.

What skills, talents, and passions has God given you to support a big vision for your God-given mission?

YOUR VISION WILL BE REVEALED OVER TIME

I mentioned that you'll need to remain flexible as you develop your vision for your personal, God-given mission. Let me explain why.

I like the GPS I have in my car. The map on it shows me exactly how to get from where I am to where I want to go. I don't have to guess how long it will take me to get from my house to the store, how fast I am allowed to drive, and how many turns I will need to make.

Having a vision for your future isn't like having a GPS in your car. You can and should make long-term plans, but God will never give you every detail about your future. You won't be able to see the entire "map" of your vision up front. Only a few of the main intersections will be marked. Perhaps He has revealed that your mission is to help Him fulfill His purposes in the world by ministering to children in the slums of Nairobi, Kenya. However, you don't know all the details or how they will play out. That's okay. It's by God's design that you don't know everything.

Your vision to support your mission must flow out of your relationship with God. Apart from Him you can do nothing (John 15:5). You cannot be the focus of your vision; Jesus must be.

God's goal is not for you to be Super Christian and become independent in your mission. You have been called to be a co-laborer with Christ (1 Corinthians 3:9). Do you remember that He desires an intimate relationship with you?

He will leverage everything in your life—including the missing pieces of your vision—to encourage you to grow closer to Him.

He wants you to lean on Him for what you don't understand. Therefore, He will press the issue of faith with you by not revealing everything ahead of time. He will leave some of the details out. That way, when you do succeed, you will give Him the glory. So plan your vision, believe big, but remain flexible as God leads you down the road you can't see ahead.

To close this chapter, let me remind you of a critical truth: When a vision begins with God, the goal of the vision will be to glorify God. But when a vision begins with *us* and *our* ideas, then the goal will be to glorify ourselves. Your vision to support your mission must flow out of your relationship with God. Apart from Him you can do nothing (John 15:5). You cannot be the focus of your vision; Jesus must be.

In the last chapter of this book, I want to share something with you that you may not have thought a lot about. There is one thing that makes pursuing your personal mission from God even more exciting than experiencing maximum fulfillment and joy in this life—and that is experiencing ultimate fulfillment.

Chapter Eight

Ultimate Fulfillment

It Will Matter In Heaven What You Do on the Earth

Imagine that NASA was so impressed with your first space voyage that they invite you on another unique trip. But this one is going to be longer because the engineers at Space Command have developed a way to leverage the speed of light so that you can travel forever and never die. To get this "anti-aging effect" you will have to zip around Betelgeuse, Alpha Centauri, and in and out of the Milky Way and the other 100 million galaxies without ever stopping. The thought of never dying thrills you, so you suit up, take a deep breath, step into your rocket, and start your forever journey.

TIME IS SHORT AND ETERNITY IS LONG

It's hard to imagine zipping around the planets forever because everything in our world has an expiration date. The milk in your refrigerator has an expiration date; your car registration has an expiration date, and even your body has an expiration date. You may have heard people say, "Nothing lasts forever." Well, nothing *on earth* lasts forever.

But three things *will* last forever: God's Word, eternity—and you.

Yes, one day your body or "earth suit" will give out and you will slip out of it like a pair of pajamas. The breath of God in you will return to God and you will meet your Maker. Paul said, "...as long we are at home in the body we are away from the Lord" (2 Corinthians 5:8).

You will meet the One who created Betelgeuse, the majestic Rocky Mountains—and gave His life on the cross for your sins. In that moment, the opportunities you had to make a difference for Christ and fulfill His purposes in the world will be gone, never to be recovered. Your moments, swallowed up in time.

That may not seem like a big deal because the earth and all its troubles will be a distant memory. After all, if you are a Christian, you will slide into eternity in bliss and nothing that you did on earth will matter in heaven anyway, right? Wrong. If you are in Christ, true, your sins have been forgiven and your punishment has been paid for, but *everything* good you did on the earth will matter in a big way in heaven.

In his book *A Life God Rewards*, Bruce Wilkinson writes,

> *Have you ever sat, eyes glued to the television watching the Olympic awards ceremony with tears streaming down your cheeks? I have. There is something about the scene that pulls at a person's heart.*
>
> *Your favorite athlete climbs the steps of the awards platform, her national anthem fills the stadium, her nation's flag waves in the spotlight. Her years of sweat and self-denial have paid off. She has finished her race. And she has won. Now, as thousands applaud, an Olympic official drapes a medal around her neck.*

One day you and I will have our own rewards ceremony in eternity. The halls of heaven will ring with praise and celebration. Witnesses from every nation and every generation will watch with eager anticipation. Even angels will pause.

When your time on earth is over, if you are a Christ follower, it will be your turn to stand on the platform to receive your rewards for what you have done on the earth.

When your time on earth is over, if you are a Christ follower, it will be your turn to stand on the platform to receive your rewards for what you have done on the earth.

Second Corinthians 5:10 says, "For we must all appear before the judgment seat of Christ, so that each of us may receive what is due us for the things done while in the body, whether good or bad."

EVERY SECOND COUNTS

I want to encourage you. You have learned that you can experience fulfillment through a relationship with Christ and by using your unique skills, talents, and passions for a personal mission to help God accomplish His purposes in the world. But God also wants you to experience ultimate fulfillment in heaven by receiving eternal rewards. I urge you: Don't waste your precious time on interests and endeavors that do not have eternal impact for Christ. Time is fleeting.

When I wake each morning and walk to the bathroom to brush my teeth, I see a little motivational quote next to the sink that reminds me that I don't have long to make an impact for Jesus. It says, "Every Second Counts." I try to remember to ask myself the question: *What will I do today that will matter in eternity?*

> *I urge you: Don't waste your precious time on interests and endeavors that do not have eternal impact for Christ. Time is fleeting.*

THE ONLY INVESTMENT THAT MATTERS IS WHAT GOD VALUES

When you were growing up did your parents say, "If you get an *A*, I'll give you a dollar"? If so, then you could tell what they valued by what they rewarded. It's the same way with God. You can tell what He values by what He rewards. And what He rewards are the only investments that really matter.

So far we have learned that God values 1) Intimacy with His creation 2) Being glorified 3) Evangelism 4) Discipleship and 5) Caring for the poor and needy. What better way to invest in what God values than through accomplishing your personal mission?

Specifically, here is an additional list of what God values and therefore, rewards.

» God will reward you for seeking Him through spiritual acts such as fasting and praying. (Matthew 6:6, Hebrews 11:6)

» God will reward you for submitting to your employer as a faithful steward. (Matthew 24:45-47; Ephesians 6:8, and Colossians 3:22-24)

» God will reward you for self-denial in His service. (Matthew 16:24-27)

» God will reward you for serving those in need in His name. (Mark 9:41)

» God will reward you for suffering for His name and reputation. (Luke 6:22-23)

» God will reward you for sacrifices you make for Him.

(Luke 6:35; Matthew 19:29)

» God will reward you for sharing your time, talent, and treasure to further His Kingdom. (Matthew 6:3-4; 1 Timothy 6:18-19)

How can you leverage your skills, talents, and passions to make a difference in eternity? Will you waste the time that you have been given on things that don't last? Every second of your life is an opportunity to invest your life in what God values and store up for yourself treasures in heaven (Matthew 6:19-20).

When your life is over, will you experience ultimate fulfillment in heaven when you receive rewards and you hear God say, "Well done?" Or will you be filled with regret?

When your life is over, will you experience ultimate fulfillment ? Or will you be filled with regret?

The choice is yours.

BLUEPRINT FOR LIFE

Visit us online for free resources and daily devotionals to help you live a life of purpose in light of eternity!

www.blueprintforlife.com

Join the conversation on Facebook and Twitter!

Discover the *Life*
You Were Born to *Live*.

BLUEPRINT FOR L*i*FE
STUDY KIT

What would it look like if your *passion* (what you really get excited about), your *giftedness* (what you're really good at), and your *calling* (your unique purpose in life) were perfectly aligned?

Blueprint for Life helps you identify and design a strategic life plan—a personal blueprint for your life—and create intentional action steps to experience the life you were born to live!

Join the conversation on Facebook and Twitter!